This book of prayers is for

_____

who began to use it on _____.

I was born to _____

on _____ in _____.

I was claimed for Christ in holy baptism

on _____ in the church of _____.

My godparents are

_____

My name was chosen because _____

_____

I received this book from

_____

BLESSINGS AND PRAYERS

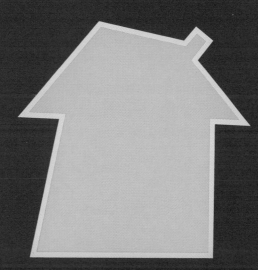

For Children Who Are Beginning to Pray with the Whole Church

Art by Judy Jarrett

Liturgy Training Publications

Acknowledgments

Excerpts from the English translation of *The Liturgy of the Hours* © 1974, International Committee on English in the Liturgy, Inc. (ICEL); excerpts from the English translation of *A Book of Prayers* © 1982, ICEL; excerpts from the *Order of Christian Funerals* © 1985, ICEL; excerpts from the English translation of *Book of Blessings* © 1988, ICEL; the English translation of Psalms 23, 121, and 148 from the *Liturgical Psalter* © 1994, ICEL. All rights reserved.

This book has been edited by Gabe Huck. Deborah Bogaert was the production editor. The design and typesetting is by Jill Smith with production assistance from Mark Hollopeter. The two typefaces are Improv and Bodoni. The book was printed and bound in the U.S.A.

Copyright © 1994, Archdiocese of Chicago: Liturgy Training Publications, 1800 North Hermitage Avenue, Chicago IL 60622-1101; 1-800-933-1800; FAX 1-800-933-7094.

All rights reserved.

ISBN 1-56854-062-0 (casebound) BLESS
ISBN 1-56854-105-8 (paper) PBLESS

Contents

About Praying with Children
page 6

Night Prayers

pages

8
16
26
28
30
46

Sign of the Cross
page 8

Meal Prayers
pages 20, 22

On Birthdays
pages 34, 36

Prayers for the Dead   pages 38, 40

Litany of the Saints
page 42

Hail Mary
page 16

Songs
Praise God from whom all blessings flow   page 24
Be present at our table, Lord   page 25
Amen   page 48

Our Father
page 10

Before Reading the Bible   page 18

Short Prayers
page 44

Blessing
page 46

Psalms
Psalm 23: The Lord is my shepherd   page 40
Psalm 148: Praise the Lord!   page 15
Psalm 121: If I look to the mountains   page 35

Glory to the Father
page 32

Morning Prayers
pages 8, 12, 14

About Praying with Children

Many of the blessings and prayers in this book have been taken from Catholic Household Blessings and Prayers. *This is a book prepared by the United States Bishops' Committee on the Liturgy. The bishops intended that book for use in every Catholic household. The following is adapted from the Foreword and the Introduction to* Catholic Household Blessings and Prayers:

Prayer must happen in the "little churches" — the households, the families — if the Sunday assembly is to become a community of prayer. The Vatican Council taught that our full participation in the liturgy "is the primary and indispensable source from which the faithful are to derive the true Christian Spirit" (Constitution on the Sacred Liturgy, #14). How can that spirit come to fill and give shape to our lives unless it is there in our prayers day by day? ¶ From one generation to the next, we must learn, hold dear, and hand on the words and gestures, the songs and scriptures of our faith. At the altar on Sunday, at table and at bedside all week, we learn throughout our lives who we are: the Body of Christ. ¶ We address a special word to parents. Some of you grew up with such words and ways of prayer. Some did not. All of us, whatever our background, are still learning to pray, still learning to be Christians. Learn well some of the daily prayers, some of the blessings for ordinary and special times. Begin to pray beside your children even when they are very young. Pray in your own words, by all means, but pray especially the words of the church. Pray because you yourself need to pray. Then, as your children grow, invite them into this prayer. Bless them each night. Pray at table with them each evening. Let them hear you singing the songs of faith and reading the holy scriptures. Let them know that fasting and almsgiving, care for the poor and the sick, and daily intercession for justice and for peace are what you hold most dear. ¶ These blessings and prayers are the ordinary ways learned day by day, season by season. They are learned at home, learned alone or learned as part of a family. They are not luxuries, pieties for the few, but are the fibers that bind baptized persons to church, to Christ, and to each other. Without them, we drift. Without them, the notion of being a church is lost to us. These prayers we take with reverence for all the generations that have shaped them for us. We will give something of ourselves to these prayers, something that they yet lack, something that can form Christians in our time and place. Then we will hand them on, for they are not finally ours. They belong to this communion of saints in which we walk and in which our children and their children may also walk.

This small book is for the child. First the pictures, then the words, will bring something to the child's own gift of wonder and prayer. Each page can be a story and a prayer as the child and the adult together look at the pictures and together say the words. Some words are really movements of the body, like the sign of the cross; it may have words or be in silence. Even the tiny "Amen" on page 48 is a prayer: "Let it be so!" it means, or just "Yes!" The words of the three psalms call for some visiting about each line. Some of the morning prayers and the meal prayers and night prayers are to be memorized, learned "by heart," so that they can be there each day to go with our rising, dressing, washing, eating, and again coming to rest. There are pages where the children can record birthdays, the names of people they pray for each day, and the names of those who have died. On the very first page of this book is a place for the child's own name and for writing down how this child came into the church and received a name.

One day the child will outgrow this book, but not its prayers. Our scriptures say that parents are to teach God's word to their children "when you rise up and when you lie down, when you sit in your house and when you walk by the way." This is our joy and the promise of God's blessing.

When we wake up in the morning and when we go to bed at night, we make the sign of the cross and say:

In the name of

the Father, and of

the Son, and of the

Holy Spirit.

Amen.

Our Father, who art in heaven,
hallowed be thy name;
thy kingdom come;
thy will be done on earth as it is in heaven.
Give us this day our daily bread;
and forgive us our trespasses
as we forgive those who trespass against us;
and lead us not into temptation,
but deliver us from evil.
Amen.

Here is another way to pray the

...Our Father.

Our Father in heaven,
hallowed be your name,
your kingdom come,
your will be done,
on earth as in heaven.
Give us today our daily bread.
Forgive us our sins
as we forgive those who sin against us.
Save us from the time of trial
and deliver us from evil.
For the kingdom, the power, and the glory are yours,
now and for ever.
Amen.

In the morning, we make a small cross on our lips and say:

Lord, open my lips,
and my mouth will proclaim your praise.

We pray in the morning when we open our eyes, when we get out of bed, when we get dressed, when we go outside:

Blessed are you, Lord, God of all creation:
you open the eyes of the blind.

Blessed are you, Lord, God of all creation:
you raise up those who are bowed down.

Blessed are you, Lord, God of all creation:
you clothe the naked.

Blessed are you, Lord, God of all creation:
you guide my footsteps.

We pray this psalm to begin the day and at other happy times.

Praise the Lord!
Across the heavens,
from the heights,
all you angels, heavenly beings,
sing praise, sing praise!

Sun and moon, glittering stars,
sing praise, sing praise.
Highest heavens, rain clouds,
sing praise, sing praise.

Praise God's name,
whose word called you forth
and fixed you in place for ever
by eternal decree.

Let there be praise:
from depths of the earth,
from creatures of the deep.

Fire and hail, snow and mist,
storms, winds,
mountains, hills,
fruit trees and cedars,
wild beasts and tame,
snakes and birds,

princes, judges,
rulers, subjects,
men, women,
old and young,
praise, praise the holy name,
this name beyond all names.

God's splendor above the earth,
above the heavens,
gives strength to the nation,
glory to the faithful,
a people close to the Lord.
Israel, let there be praise!

Psalm 148

We pray this anytime, but especially at noon and at bedtime:

Hail Mary, full of grace,

the Lord is with you!

Blessed are you among women,

and blessed is the fruit of your womb, Jesus.

Holy Mary, mother of God,

pray for us sinners,

now and at the hour of our death.

Amen.

Your promises are sweet to taste, sweeter than honey.

Your word is a lamp for my steps,
a light for my path.

19

Before eating and drinking, we make the sign of the cross and say:

Bless us, O Lord, and these your gifts
which we are about to receive from your goodness.
Through Christ our Lord.

Amen.

Another prayer before meals:

All the world hopes in you, O Lord,
that you will give us food in our hunger.
You open wide your hand
and we are filled with good things.

After eating, we say:

Let all your works praise you, Lord.

Let all your people bless you.

We give you thanks for all your gifts, almighty God,

living and reigning now and for ever. Amen.

Other prayers after eating:

Blessed be the Lord,
of whose bounty we have received
and by whose goodness we live.

The poor shall eat and shall have their fill.
Those who long for the Lord shall give God praise.
May their hearts live for ever.

23

This is a song for any day:

Praise God from whom all blessings flow.
Praise God, all creatures here below.
Praise God above, ye heavenly host.
Praise Father, Son and Holy Ghost.

This prayer may be sung before or after eating:

Be present at our table, Lord.

Be here and everywhere adored.

Thy creatures bless and grant that we

May feast in Paradise with thee.

Especially in the evening, we pray for all the world:

Remember, Lord, all of us in this house.

    Lord, have mercy.

Remember, Lord, all who love us.

    Lord, have mercy.

Remember, Lord, our friends.

    Lord, have mercy.

Remember, Lord, every person who is hungry.

    Lord, have mercy.

Remember, Lord, all the children in the world.

    Lord, have mercy.

Remember, Lord, all the people who are sick or unhappy.

    Lord, have mercy.

Remember, Lord, all the people who are away from home.

    Lord, have mercy.

Remember, Lord, everyone who has died.

    Lord, have mercy.

We add to these whatever else we ask God to remember.

Here are the names of people we pray for:

In bed at night, or kneeling by the bed, we pray some of these prayers:

Visit this house,
we beg you, Lord.
May your holy angels dwell here
to keep us in peace,
and may your blessing be always
upon us.

Angel sent by God to guide me,
be my light and walk beside me;
be my guardian and protect me;
on the paths of life direct me.

Other prayers at night:

Now I lay me down to sleep,

I pray the Lord my soul to keep.

Four corners to my bed,

Four angels there aspread:

Two to foot and two to head,

And four to carry me when I'm dead.

If any danger come to me,

Sweet Jesus Christ deliver me.

And if I die before I wake,

I pray the Lord my soul to take.

C

Mary, mother whom we bless,

full of grace and tenderness,

defend me from the devil's power

and greet me in my dying hour.

Sometimes we stand and bow deeply when we say:

Glory to the Father, and to the Son, and to the Holy Spirit:

as it was in the beginning, is now, and will be for ever.

The day of my birth:

_____

On my birthday, I give thanks to God and I pray:

If I look to the mountains,
will they come to my aid?
My help is the Lord,
who made earth and the heavens.

May God, ever wakeful,
keep you from stumbling;
the guardian of Israel
neither rests nor sleeps.

God shields you,
a protector by your side.
The sun shall not harm you by day
nor the moon at night.

God shelters you from evil,
securing your life.
God watches over you near and far,
now and always.

Psalm 121

When someone celebrates a birthday, we can place our hands on this person and pray this blessing:

May God, in whose presence our ancestors walked, bless you.
Amen.

May God, who has been your shepherd from birth until now, keep you.
Amen.

May God, who saves you from all harm, give you peace.
Amen.

Here are the Birthdays of people I know

We pray for those who have died:

Eternal rest grant unto them, O Lord.
And let perpetual light shine upon them.

May they rest in peace.
Amen.

May their souls and the souls of all the faithful departed, through the mercy of God, rest in peace.
Amen.

These are people who have died.
I pray for them.

We pray this psalm often, especially on sad days:

The Lord is my shepherd,
I need nothing more.
You give me rest in green meadows,
setting me near calm waters,
where you revive my spirit.

You guide me along sure paths,
you are true to your name.
Though I should walk in death's dark valley,
I fear no evil with you by my side,
your shepherd's staff to comfort me.

You spread a table before me
as my foes look on.
You soothe my head with oil;
my cup is more than full.

Goodness and love will tend me
every day of my life.
I will dwell in the house of the Lord
as long as I shall live.

Psalm 23

We ask all the angels and the saints to

Pray for us.

Lawrence & Stephen

Joseph

Clare & Francis

John the Baptist

Adam & Eve

Mary, Mother of God

Joachim & Ann

Cecilia & Lucy

Michael and all Angels

Deborah & Ruth

Abraham & Sarah

42

Francis Xavier

Thérèse

Agnes & Barbara

Rose of Lima

Mary Magdalene

Martin de Porres

Andrew & James

Scholastica & Benedict

Elizabeth Ann Seton

Jeremiah & Daniel

Zechariah & Elizabeth

All holy men and women,

Pray for us.

Kateri Tekakwitha

Felicity & Perpetua

Patrick & Brigid

These are short prayers
for many different times:

Praised
BE
Jesus Christ.

THANKS be to **GOD**.

Glory
to
God in the highest.

When going away from home or when going to bed at night, we give each other a blessing. A young child may learn one line of this to bless a younger brother or sister.

May the Lord bless us and keep us.

May the face of the Lord shine on us and be kind to us.

May the Lord turn toward us and give us peace.

48